D1760143

Profiles

MAYA MOORE

BARBARA LOWELL

WORLD BOOK

This World Book edition of *Maya Moore*
is published by agreement between
Black Rabbit Books and World Book, Inc.
© 2020 Black Rabbit Books,
2140 Howard Dr. West,
North Mankato, MN 56003 U.S.A.
World Book, Inc.,
180 North LaSalle St., Suite 900,
Chicago, IL 60601 U.S.A.

Jennifer Besel & Marysa Storm, editors; Grant Gould, designer;
Omay Ayres, photo researcher

Library of Congress Control Number: 2018045158

ISBN: 978-0-7166-3957-2

Printed in the United States. 2/19

Image Credits

Alamy: Cal Sport Media, 8–9;
ZUMA Press, Inc., Cover, 12, 28–29
(bkgd), 32; AP Images: David Goldman, 15;
Jason Getz, 11 (top); china.org.cn: China.org.cn,
20–21; commons.wikimedia.org: Joe Bielawa, 1; fiba.
basketball: FIBA, 27; Getty: Adam Bettcher, 24–25; Andy
King, 4–5; Tim Clayton – Corbis, 18 (btm); Newscom:
Anthony Nesmith/Cal Sport Media, 6–7; Darrell Walker/
Icon SMI 945, 26 (top); Kyndell Harkness/MCT/Newscom, 26
(middle); MIKE SEGAR/REUTERS, 18 (top); Mingo Nesmith/
Icon Sportswire DIL, 16–17; Shutterstock: Brent Hofacker, 9;
Slavoljub Pantelic, 3; vasosh, 31; stack.com: Brian Sabin, 22;
starsunfolded.com: Stars Unfolded, 11 (btm); the-boneyard.
com: MilfordHusky, 13; thedrum.com: RTVV, 8;
twitter.com: Greg Morrisey, 26 (btm)
Every effort has been made to contact copyright hold-
ers for material reproduced in this book. Any
omissions will be rectified in subsequent
printings if notice is given to the
publisher.

CONTENTS

CHAPTER 1

A Talented PLAYER

It was the 2017 WNBA finals. Maya Moore's team, the Minnesota Lynx, faced the Los Angeles Sparks. Both teams had won two games. Whichever team won this game would win the championship.

With 30 seconds left in the game, Moore had the ball. She raced up the court. She jumped and let the ball fly. Swoosh. It sailed through the hoop. Moore's basket **secured** her fourth WNBA championship win.

One of the Greats

Moore plays **forward**. During games, she shows **skill** with quick moves. She makes many baskets. Moore is one of the best players in the WNBA.

Moore wears number 23. She chose it because Michael Jordan wore it. She also picked it because LeBron James wears it.

FUN FACTS

ENJOYS PLAYING DRUMS

LIKES TO READ

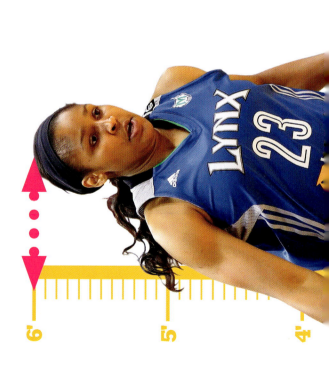

6'

5'

4'

NAMED AFTER THE POET MAYA ANGELOU

favorite flavor of ice cream is mint chocolate chip

6 feet (1.8 meters) tall

2'

0

CHAPTER 2

Moore's Early

Moore was born on June 11, 1989. From an early age, she loved to run and jump. Moore played many sports as a kid. But she liked basketball the most. She joined her first basketball team in elementary school. Moore spent hours practicing.

Moore was raised by a single mother. The two have a very close relationship.

Moore helped UConn to
a 90-game winning streak.

Winning Big

Moore was an outstanding player at Collins Hill High School. She •••••••• helped her team win three state titles.

In college, Moore helped the University of Connecticut to two NCAA titles. With Moore, the school's four-year record was 150 wins and four losses. Moore scored 3,036 points with the team.

CHAPTER 3

Going

In 2011, Moore joined the Lynx. She was the number one WNBA **draft** pick. She led the team to its first championship that year. Lynx fans were **thrilled**. Moore became the 2011 WNBA **Rookie** of the Year.

Moore and the Lynx kept winning too. They have won three more championships.

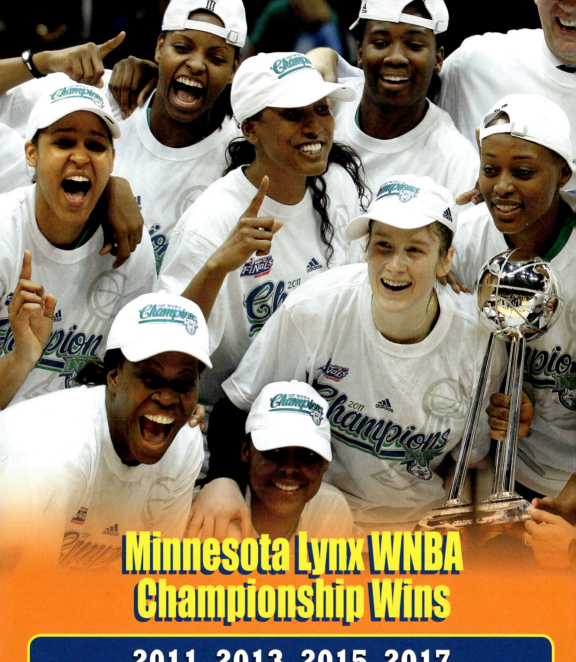

Minnesota Lynx WNBA Championship Wins

2011, 2013, 2015, 2017

Runners-Up

2012, 2016

(through 2018)

games played
271

number of free throws
890

number of 2-pointers
1,252

number of 3-pointers
530

number of steals 449

total points 4,984

Winning Gold

Growing up, Moore watched the Olympics on TV. She hoped one day she'd play for Team USA. And she did. Moore played in the 2012 and 2016 Olympics. She helped Team USA win a gold medal each year.

Around the World

Moore plays for the Lynx. But during its off-season, she's played for teams in other countries. Moore has played several seasons with the Shanxi Flame. It's a team in China. Moore helped the team win three championships. And Moore doesn't even speak Chinese.

In one game with the Flame, Moore scored 60 points.

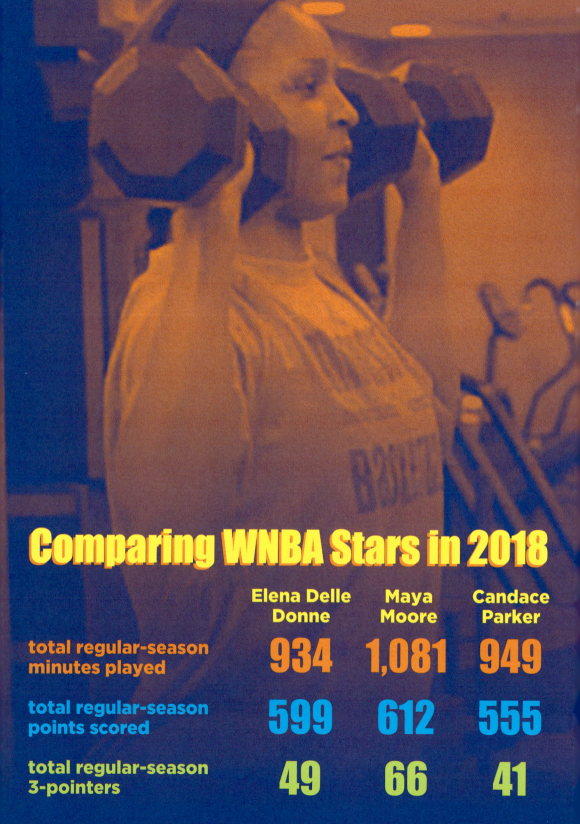

Comparing WNBA Stars in 2018

	Elena Delle Donne	Maya Moore	Candace Parker
total regular-season minutes played	934	1,081	949
total regular-season points scored	599	612	555
total regular-season 3-pointers	49	66	41

CHAPTER 4

On and Off the COURT

Moore spends hours practicing her skills. She exercises to keep her body strong. Moore drinks lots of water and eats lots of vegetables. She stays away from dairy and foods with added sugar. Moore is always ready to play her best.

Giving Back

Moore believes in helping others. She is part of the Kid Power program. This program helps kids be active. When they're active, kids earn points. When they earn enough points, Kid Power donates food to hungry kids.

Moore also teaches basketball skills to kids. She has a basketball camp. It's called the Maya Moore Academy.

Moore's Most Valuable Player
Awards

2013
WNBA Finals **MVP**

2014
WNBA MVP

2015, 2017,
and 2018 WNBA
All-Star Game MVP

2014
FIBA World
Championship MVP

A Bright Future

Moore is an accomplished athlete and amazing teammate. From high school to pro basketball, she's won many championships and awards. She has a bright future ahead of her. Her fans can't wait to see what she does next.

TIMELINE

1989
born in Missouri

2012
helps team win gold
at Olympics

1980

2011
Lynx drafts Moore &
named WNBA Rookie of the Year

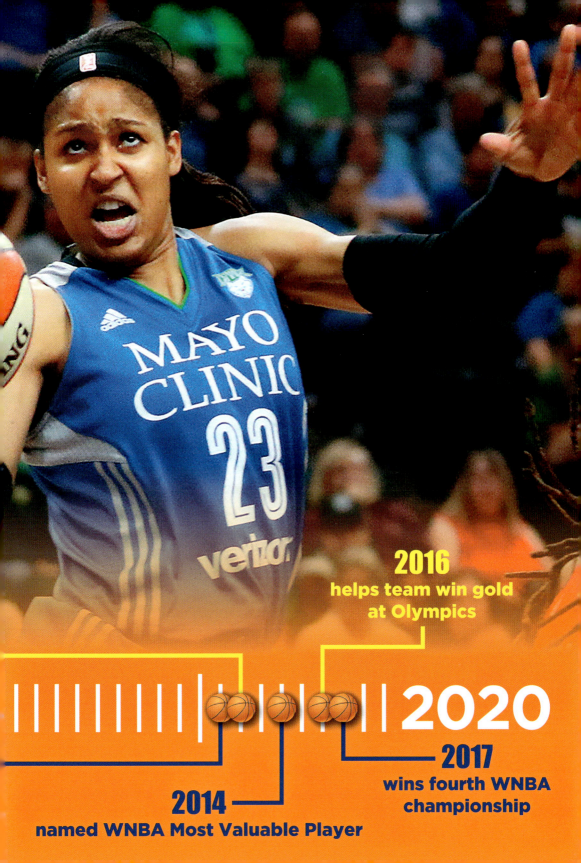

2016
helps team win gold
at Olympics

2020

2017
wins fourth WNBA
championship

2014
named WNBA Most Valuable Player

draft (DRAFT)—a system in which new players are chosen for professional teams; it also means to pick a player for a professional team through a specialized system.

forward (FOR-wurd)—a basketball player whose main job is to move the ball toward the opponent's basket and try to score

MVP—an award given to the best player in the league each season; MVP stands for most valuable player.

rookie (ROOK-ee)—a first-year player

secure (suh-KEYR)—free from risk of loss

skill (SKIL)—the ability to do something that comes from training, experience, or practice

steal (STEEL)—to take from another player

streak (STREEK)—a series of something

thrill (THRIL)—to cause someone to feel very excited or happy

BOOKS

Clausen-Grace, Nicki, and Jeff Grace. *Basketball Superstars.* Got Game. Mankato, MN: Black Rabbit Books, 2018.

Raum, Elizabeth. *Maya Moore.* Pro Sports Biographies. Mankato, MN: Amicus High Interest/Amicus Ink, 2018.

Scheff, Matt. *Maya Moore.* Biggest Names in Sports. Lake Elmo, MN: Focus Readers, 2019.

WEBSITES

10 Questions with ... Maya Moore
**www.sikids.com/si-kids/2016/01/12/
10-questions-12**

Maya Moore
www.wnba.com/player/maya-moore/

Maya Moore – Official Website of Maya Moore
mayamoore.com

INDEX